# Post-Traumatically Stressed Feminist
## Survivors Reclaiming Their Truths

*Love + Revolution*

### Edited by Darci McFarland

Cover designed by Callie Garp of Fabulously Feminist

For all of the survivors out there.
You are not alone.

# Introduction

Post-Traumatically Stressed Feminist is a collection of stories, poems, visual art, and social commentary on Post-Traumatic Stress Disorder and Post-Traumatic Growth. Feminist artists and writers from various social and geographical locations have contributed to its birth – all are survivors of trauma.

We created Post-Traumatically Stressed Feminist to amplify the voices of survivors and to build ourselves a platform for healing and collective action. Because the majority of resources that do exist for people with Post-Traumatic Stress Disorder center veterans who have served in combat or people seeking immediate assistance leaving an abusive relationship, there are millions of people - people who have previously been in abusive relationships, people who have experienced childhood abuse, people who have experienced sexual assault or violence, people who have unexpectedly lost a parent or child - who never get the support and resources they need.

We created Post-Traumatically Stressed Feminist to educate friends, relatives, and loved ones about PTSD and the effects of trauma on one's life. Because trauma varies and humans vary, no experience is the same. Each individual person experiences different symptoms in different degrees. It's crucial to remember that certain behaviors and characteristics are just that – symptoms – not who your loved one actually is. Patience and empathy is key. I promise, we are trying.

We created Post-Traumatically Stressed Feminist to explore the social systems that cause trauma: misogyny, white supremacy, homophobia, transphobia, etc. (Etc. not because they are less important, but because they are not explored in this book.)

They are all pervasive and interconnected. For many of us, survival includes making sure fewer people have to live through what we have lived through.

We created Post-Traumatically Stressed Feminist for survivors. To remind them that they are not alone – that there are millions of us – who don't look anything like the soldiers we see on TV.

We created Post-Traumatically Stressed Feminist because we need something to hold on to while we are in the trenches of our trauma. We need to be reminded that we can still create beautiful and powerful things.

[Content Warning: The work in this book is likely to be triggering as it contains discussion of sexual violence, loss, self-harm, miscarriage, and various other traumatic experiences.]

# Table of Contents

# Dear Survivor

Heather Stout

Dear Survivor,

First and foremost: I believe you, I believe you, I believe you. I know you have nothing to gain from being open and honest about what happened to you, except peace of mind. I know the false rape myth is overwhelmingly accepted even though there is a 2.7 million to 1 chance[1] you'll be falsely accused, meaning a person is more likely to win the lottery or be drafted by the NFL or killed by a damn comet than ever be falsely accused. I know a 2013 study out of the UK[2] showed the percentage of false reports to be 0.6% overall. I know you may not have a police report or a court document as evidence because you were afraid of what would happen if you went forward, but it doesn't mean it didn't happen. Everyone knows the rapist is innocent until proven guilty and that the victim is the real defendant, that's what you told the therapist was the reason you didn't go to the dean. Like many college kids, you didn't report because you didn't think you could handle it. I know the overwhelming majority of rapes are vastly underreported due to the same fear, and I believe those survivors, too.

Rape culture excuses what happens and, when we do report, shifts the blame on us. There are countless high-profile examples of just how little respect survivors are given. Certain politicians and pundits actively blame survivors for the impact rape culture has on us. And it's not just the court of public opinion who doesn't believe survivors, cops don't[3] because they don't understand the aftereffects of trauma. But rape culture is a liar-- what happened was NOT your fault. What you were wearing doesn't matter (a tunic and leggings) and what you were doing doesn't matter (God forbid a 21-year-old college kid drink). You thought about being raped in your own bed when Emma Sulkowicz carried her mattress around Columbia University. You had no reason to be afraid of being alone in your apartment with your rapist. You could not have known what your rapist was planning to do when y'all met up; they were your friend and you trusted them. At least 7/10 sexual assaults are perpetrated by a non-stranger,[4] you were not alone in believing you were safe. It was not your fault, it was not your fault, it was not your fault-- it is never ANY survivor's fault.

Despite knowing all these things, despite educating yourself about feminism and rape culture, despite knowing there is nothing a survivor could do to prevent what happens to us, you still sometimes blamed yourself (and even now you sometimes do). And you couldn't stand seeing your rapist around campus. Despite having a circle of support (not every survivor is so lucky), you looked for ways to cope[5] with that overwhelming self-guilt. You knew survivors of rape are 13.4 times more likely to develop two or more alcohol related problems and 26 times more likely to have two or more serious drug abuse-related problems,[6] but you still trusted alcohol.

Nobody will ever know the severity of your drinking problem. You just felt so broken! The only way you could sleep was drinking until you were blackout drunk because it meant you didn't have to dream about what happened. Your friends and family tried to reach out, but you couldn't handle acknowledging your preferred (maladaptive) coping mechanism was slowly killing you. Sometimes the only way you knew you were alive was feeling the burn of whiskey going down your throat. There are some things you cannot express; you do not have the words to illuminate the depths of your loneliness or the weight of despair you felt in your bones.

But one night you watched First Wives Club and when Stockard Channing stepped off that balcony you looked at the drink in your hand, the same thing she'd had, and started crying. You thought about Alice Sebold's line in Lucky, "No one can pull anyone back from anywhere. You save yourself or you remain unsaved." You thought about all the survivors you know and how damn strong they are, whether or not they know it themselves. You poured out your drink, and you haven't had another drop since.

You are no less of a person because you were raped. Sometimes people don't know how to handle your willingness (or hesitation) to share details. You know they mean well, but platitudes don't always help. I personally think every survivor who tells their story is an activist. We deserve the power to control the narrative surrounding rape culture. By telling our story, we are making those in our lives realize they know someone who has been directly impacted by rape. We make it real. The stories other survivors tell me both grieve and embolden me, reminding me I am not alone in my struggle. Every survivor I meet makes me want to do *more*. But even those survivors who don't talk about what happened are radical to me. That's okay, there is no "right" way to be a survivor. Your experience is still valid. Your feelings are still valid. You may not be ready to talk about it for years, you may never be ready to talk about it all.

Our community is not a monolith and we cannot dictate how any other survivor lives, but we all have this in common: we did not deserve what happened to us and we are never alone. You are not "a stronger person" after what happened, you have always been strength incarnate. Some days are harder than others— the "rapeiversary" or their birthday or maybe you were triggered by something and end up completely shutting down— but you are still here. You are not now, nor have you ever been, broken. You are still picking up the pieces. You are still fighting. You are still here. We are powerful and capable of immense love. The road to recovery may be long, but you can do it. We all can. We all will.

I believe your story and I believe in your strength. You are loved, survivor.

Love,
Heather Stout

---

1. Charles Clymer, "5 Things More Likely To Happen To You Than Being Falsely Accused Of Rape," Buzzfeed, http://www.buzzfeed.com/charlesclymer/5-things-more-likely-to-happen-to-you-than-being-f-fmeu
2. Alison Levitt, Charging Perverting the Course of Justice and Wasting Police Time in Cases Involving Allegedly False Rape and Domestic Violence Allegations: Joint Report to the Director of Public Prosecutions, http://www.cps.gov.uk/publications/research/perverting_course_of_justice_march_2013.pdf
3. Rebecca Ruiz, "Why Don't Cops Believe Rape Victims?" Slate, http://www.slate.com/articles/news_and_politics/jurisprudence/2013/06/why_cops_don_t_believe_rape_victims_and_how_brain_science_can_solve_the.html
4. "Perpetrators of Sexual Violence: Statistics," RAINN, https://rainn.org/statistics/perpetrators-sexual-violence
5. "Substance Abuse," RAINN, https://rainn.org/articles/substance-abuse "Mental Health Issues," National Criminal Justice Reverence Service, https://www.ncjrs.gov/ovc_archives/ncvrw/2005/pg5n.html

# Sexy, NOT Sexual

Darcy Wilkins

I

My mother tells me that I was being ogled by men by the time I was four years old. I was a very active child, so I had good musculature and enviable posture. Four years old was about the time she noticed men watching me wherever I went, and also about the time men seemed to start deciding it would be okay to discuss my body with her. It became even more imperative not to let me out of her sight after that.

I remember being maybe five, walking my grandmother's dog up and down in front of her house, always in view of the big picture window, and being approached by a youth in his late teens or early twenties. He asked me things like, "How old are you?" "Do you live here?" "Does your dog bite?" Finally he told me to call him when I turned 18. I didn't know what that meant at the time, but I kind of felt what it meant.

I must have been only ten, on a road trip with my parents, watching Disney movies and playing with my Barbies in the backseat, when we stopped at a truck stop diner to eat. We walked in, started perusing the menu at the counter, and I suddenly got an incredibly uneasy feeling. I looked around, and every single man in the establishment was turned to stare at me. Me. Not my father, not my mother (who was very curvaceous herself), but me. The wolves had caught my nubile scent. That is the very first time I remember consciously feeling the male gaze, and it crashed into me like a tidal wave.

From that minute on, I interacted in the world differently. From that minute on, I was on a stage, and if I was going to be constantly watched, I would give the audience a show.

## II

I have dozens of older male cousins, uncles, brothers, and a father, and ever since I can remember, all of the men in my life have been telling me, "Do not trust guys. Guys only want one thing from you, and you will not, under any circumstances, give it to them." Over and over and over and over, and in every way possible. As far as I can remember this is what all of my conversations with adult men were about. You know, until I was old enough for them to start asking me, "So why don't you have a boyfriend?"

These lessons and interrogations were meant to be cute, sweet, and protective. They did it out of love for me and worry for what inevitably happens to any child when they grow up. They wanted me to know that they would have my back if anyone tried to hurt me, and there is no denying that that is incredibly sweet and endearing. I would imagine that the majority of southern girls have experienced this same thing from the adult males in their lives, and it affected each and every one of us differently. But for me it ended up being a mantra that stuck with me like superglue to my fingers, and it inhibited my actions in the world as such; you can scrub and scrub, and the glue won't come off without taking a little piece of your skin with it. Or you can wait for life to wear it down, for you to shed the skin that the glue is adhered to, simply through living. Either way, it doesn't come off easily, and it makes your fingers feel like they no longer belong to you: there is a boundary now between you and the world. These male-given, man-hating diatribes made my body feel like something that didn't truly belong to me, because the underlying assumption with those assertions is that it doesn't. Since this meant there was no way I could protect my own body from any man if he wanted it, I became detached from my ownership of myself. And so every conversation with male relatives became a fresh application of glue.

Even to this day, at 27-years-old, the first thing my brothers will say to me if I make any mention of dating a guy is some variation of: "If he ever hurts you I will end his life," and though it's relatively sweet, that line of threats and promises always continues for at least ten minutes. Thus, every crush or relationship I've ever had has begun with the idea that the boy in question can, and probably will, hurt me. As a result, I became terrified, distrustful, and disdainful towards men. But not men in general. I had the men in my family and some very good male friends, all of whom I trusted implicitly, but now there was a new subset that encompassed every other man who might view me sexually. The rhetoric of the men I trusted created an entirely new category of males in my head.

I came to believe that these men, that I will call "Fem Farmers," are like pig farmers who specialize in women. First of all, they own the female body. They carefully oversee the breeding, nurturing, and growth of women. They count and weigh them, poke and prod them, manhandle and discuss them in vulgar terms, decide which of them are good for which tasks, and then funnel them into separate chutes to either be gobbled up or bred. Controlling women's bodies is their livelihood and the source of all of their profits. Women are property, and women are meat. To Fem Farmers the very core value of me was as a sexual object and nothing else. But honestly, that was a better option than to have no value at all, because that chute ends in obsolescence. So I had decided to give my audience, my overseers, what they wanted: I acted sexy, dressed sexy, walked sexy, and danced sexy. But most importantly, I talked dumb. Because in my mind all any man/boy/guy cared about is whether or not I was sexy. Because still for a great number of men, smart is not sexy.

So the number one rule of the game became: be sexy in every way possible, but never give anyone actual sex. This, I deduced, was my power. This was the way to "win" the Game of Life. Be sexy, but not sexual. Be something good to look at and you will command attention. Be something good in bed and you have given all of your power away to the men who enjoy it. Mystery and anticipation are what was actually sexy, so "giving it up" stripped away your mystery, therefore your sexiness, and thus, your power. Sex made you vulnerable, and vulnerability was not sexy. In fact, it made you prime for slaughter.

Life became a competition of Boy vs. Girl, "giving it up" was the ultimate loss, and I am ignited by a challenge. In this way "teasing" became the only option available to me: turn them on and scamper off. This got me labeled as a tease, a slut (by the girls), and a lesbian interchangeably in middle school and high school (so I guess you could say I was a triple threat?), but the most important thing to me was that I never gave it up. I was still winning the ultimate game, and that's all that mattered.

### III

I was a gregarious child, and I am a vivacious person. When I was a baby, before I could talk, if anyone around me was sad or quiet, I would fix them with an iconic smirk and belt out "HAH-HAH!" at regular intervals until anyone and everyone was laughing. In preschool I was never afraid to approach a new person for friendship. I was always the first to introduce myself to boys and girls alike, and get a game of "Pretend" going. By all accounts, throughout my childhood I was the cuddliest, huggiest, most touchy-feely little girl in the world. But around age 13 my parents began to notice I never wanted to be touched anymore. I would angrily and violently squirm away from their hands, wriggle out of anyone's lap or embrace. That of course was in large part due to the raging hormones of puberty, but I think it was also a reaction to feeling like my body was not mine, to feeling the weight of those bodily labels more heavily than the weight of my forming breasts. I love people, and people are attracted to me. But when your body is all you think you have to offer anyone, for your whole life you have been put into very specific boxes because of it, and it is changing before your eyes, you want to hide in your chrysalis until you know what the metamorphosis will leave you with.

But my body only became more sexual, of course. "Sexy" became my core identifier to the outside world and therefore "smart" was locked away in the basement. I acted dumb because if no one cared about anything but how sexy I was, if everyone was going to label me based on that, without caring about any other aspect of my person, then I wasn't going to show anyone anything but how sexy I was. No man deserved it, and no man could handle it, being the "essentially sex-driven, lizard-brained savages" I had learned and taught myself they were. Being smart was not sexy, and sexy is all I was and could be to them. It was deflection: attracting their attention to my body was a tactic for protecting my true self from the predators' notice.

But the problem is that I am smart. I got straight A's all through high school. I earned an International Baccalaureate diploma, which still remains the hardest two years of my education. I graduated from an amazing liberal arts college Summa Cum Laude and with honors in Anthropology. I love school, I love learning, and I love expressing myself in a multitude of ways, but I didn't think any men deserved that self-expression from me, because I didn't think any of them would value it for what it was truly worth. The Fem Farmers would funnel me right into the slaughter chute if they were to even suspect.

So with this big, heavy, human brain of mine, my adolescence became an exercise in over-analyzing myself and maintaining my white-knuckled clutch on the reigns of my body. When I entered college I found unprecedented relief in relinquishing those reigns to the carefree abandon of alcohol. I did not, and do not, have a problem with addiction, but I had built a wall around my life composed entirely of inhibitions, and alcohol was the toddler crashing through my Lego castle. If I was addicted to anything, it was that toddler's pure and contagious laughter as the bricks fell to the ground; but without fail, the next day while the toddler slept, I would resolutely rebuild that castle each and every time. Intelligence was packed carefully inside the walls where no one could scrutinize, and ogle, and gossip about it like they did my body, and the moat swam with (sexy, sexy) alligators to deter anyone from climbing the turrets.

However, I didn't truly realize the monstrosity of impenetrable proportions that I had built until sophomore year of college. That year, on a regular weekend, one of my dearest friends (who was a psychology major, incidentally) asked me to take a walk around campus with her to discuss something with me. I was confused and nervous, because we had never done this before and something was obviously wrong. Finally she worked up the courage to tell me that she was concerned about how I acted around, and presented myself to, men. I was completely blind-sided by this. Isn't this how you're supposed to act with men? Aren't they supposed to be kept at arm's length only, warily watched as they lustfully watched us? Like predator and prey circling each other in a stand-off that could only end in one of you losing?

...No?
Oh...

So after my intervention, I slowly and painfully started training the "dumb blonde" persona out of myself. It wasn't immediate, and it wasn't easy. It was gradual and subtle. My friends noticed, and through their encouragement I was finally beginning to believe that men could find value in my brain. I started taking to Facebook to express myself. I began small, relaying silly observations and events in my life in funny ways, and the responses I got fueled me to keep testing the waters. I gradually increased to things that seemed silly but became unexpectedly deep, and people started to be delightedly surprised with my "sneak-attack wit."

Yet, still when I crossed the stage to get my college diploma, announced with all of my honors, there was actually a split second of stunned silence from the audience before such uproarious applause that I actually gasped before sprinting to get out of the limelight. Afterwards I was bombarded by my classmates rushing up to tell me that I "won college" because they "had no idea [I was] smart!"

Well, that there was another challenge. That false perception was my own doing and I had to fix it. I have spent the last five years carefully crafting Facebook rants, musings, and observations, hitting that "post status" button and releasing my brain into the world. That has been one of the very best things for my "recovery" and I am proud of how far I've come. I am truly myself in the world now, the good, the bad, the ugly, AND the sexy, and I'm never looking back.

But that doesn't mean that years of psychological training have gone away. It doesn't mean I've scrubbed off all of the glue. The problem now was that my sexuality had always been so public that I had absolutely no idea of how to deal with it in private. In private, all of the strictly obeyed rules by which I had crafted my entire public persona didn't apply. In private I was continually sent out onto the stage without knowing any of my lines. It was like the field of play had been switched from freshly mown grass to four-feet of swamp muck.

And even though I now unabashedly own my sexiness in the public sphere, I am still a sexual object in a man's world. Cat-calling and street harassment are pervasive for all women. The fear of random acts of violence against women and rape is real and omnipresent. I have, on multiple occasions, been straight up told by both strange and familiar men, many variations of, "You look like you would be good at sex." But despite the vulgarity, at least those men are upfront about what they want. Dating these days, or the pathetic attempt at the façade of dating, can for the vast majority of my experience be boiled down to: "excuse me, Madam, I would very much like to use your body to pleasure myself. What's the going rate? A couple of rum-and-cokes? Dinner if you're feeling hard-to-get?"

Women have a lot of terrible sexual experiences. I have had a lot of terrible sexual experiences. Many men have had terrible sexual experiences as well, and I am definitely not trying to demean victims of male molestation or rape, but for women, traumatization by a sexual experience is almost considered inevitable. Yet, when I learned from my gynecologist that I myself have some psychological sexual trauma that was manifesting with physical side effects, it still shook me up more than I expected it to. I have never been violently raped, but I have typed up over thirty pages of stories of my non-consensual, scary, sad, ridiculous, and sometimes hilarious dealings with "Fem Farmers," and I think the majority of women in this great-big, blue, world could probably do the same. In fact, all of my diaries from ages seven to twenty-seven could probably have a fourth of their contents extracted and the remainder simply be renamed "My Confounding, Dumb, and Terrifying Interactions With People Who Own Penises."

So I knew I had issues with sex and men, but I didn't know it was diagnosable, and what my gynecologist finally revealed to me is that I was switching up the playing fields myself. I have the script, but I'm terrified of playing the part. Where I am the star of the half-time show on the big stadium stage, I have crippling stage fright in the intimacy of the small local theater, and I am the only person who can fix that.

## IV

It is true that my detachment from, casual disdain for, and terror of Fem Farmers throughout my life have been responses to relentless, pervasive, and both painfully subtle and outrageously aggressive, oppression by them. It's an extreme reaction to the feeling that my body puts me in a lesser category than a male body does, because I don't own mine. Somehow the Fem Farmer owns his and he also owns mine. It is the extreme reaction to the knowledge that my body can be usurped from me at any point, that all men want to seize it like a barbarian army eyeing an enemy fortress, and that that is only their nature, so it can't be helped. I have been sexualized for my entire life, and that took my sexuality away from me. But that was kind of the point, wasn't it?

I have had my ass slapped, grabbed, and fondled by males I knew and by complete strangers, in public and in private spaces, since I was 11 or 12 years old. I've had strange men try to finger me on crowded dance floors. I have had bosses and interns alike, talk to, and text me, inappropriately at work. I have been unknowingly followed home by someone whom I thought was a friend, yet accosted me outside of the building, without speaking a word, and shoved his hands into my pants before I could, in shock, squirm away and run up the stairs. Things like this have happened to me countless numbers of times in countless situations. And in probably more than 75% of cases I responded by giggling and playfully pushing the aggressor away as if we were in on some funny joke together. Why? Because as a woman, not only are you taught to always say "no," but you are also taught that when your no's don't work you just need to "not make things weird." According to a great number of people out there, my sexuality is not mine, and making a scene when a man tries to take it from me would somehow be the obscene part of that situation. My body is unclaimed territory, prime for the taking, unless I have a boyfriend of course. Men may not respect the land itself, but they do respect another man's flag shoved into it.

Speaking of boyfriends, I've had multiple best-friend's boyfriends get drunk and try to get me to kiss them, or hit on me, or grab my ass, or all of the above. In college one time I got a little too drunk at a house party, so my friend put me in bed next to her already-passed-out boyfriend; a boy I knew and trusted and that my friend obviously trusted as well. The whole reason for putting me in there with him was to make sure no random party-goer could prey upon me in my weakened state. I woke up to that boyfriend playing with my panty-line and stroking my waist and hips. But I lay there and pretended to be asleep, moving away from him as much as I could while maintaining my sleeping facade, because maybe he was sleep-fondling and I didn't want to make things weird.

"Oh you know how men are, they just can't help it!"
"They just want to show you how attractive you are, what's the big deal?"
"If you didn't want it then why were you flirting with me?"
"Maybe you shouldn't have dressed like that."
"Why didn't you just say 'no'?"

Because women are indoctrinated to not make a scene, not be hysterical or crazy, and most importantly, not to be "mean," a bitch, or "bossy." Because often times this type of thing happens to us at the hands of people we know and trust, and the event is so shocking you don't know what to do in the moment. Because saying "no" only works some of the time, and having your "no's" ignored feels like having boulders catapulted right into your castle walls. It's much easier, much more palatable for your psyche, to pretend like you're in on the plan, than to accuse someone of having an extreme and frightening power over you to make you do what they want. Womanhood, as I've known it, is about creating layers upon layers of protection around yourself; digging your moat until you suddenly find yourself to be on an island. Don't let any man get too close because he will take any opportunity to get much closer than you want him to. And you know what he'll be saying the whole time? "Don't make this weird. Don't make this weird. Don't make this weird."

So in a sense, my cousins, uncles, brothers, and father were all right. There is a lot of evidence out there that the Fem Farmers are after one thing and one thing only. That they will try to get that thing at any cost, using any tricks, without any care for what the woman actually wants. Pervasive sexism and patriarchy STILL, in 2016, can lay waste to the fortress you've built of yourself. And it's easy as women to collect all of these different oppressive experiences with men, in all of the facets of our lives, and say, simply, "well…so men just kinda suck, yeah?" But, they are as much victims of the patriarchy as we are, because they have been funneled into these roles generation after generation. Our society teaches boys from the earliest ages that femininity is derogatory ("you pansy," "you pussy," "You throw like a girl"), so how can they not come out thinking women are the lesser? And we cannot forget that where sexual predation is concerned, women are perpetrators too.

When girls are taught to only say "no," boys learn that "no" sometimes means "yes." Femininity is already devalued, as detailed above, so this doubly devalues the female "no," to the point of making "yes" obsolete. In the same vein, our society teaches that men should always want to say "yes," and if they are truly a red-blooded, virile man, there is no reason for them ever to say "no." In this way, girls learn to devalue a boy's "no" too. We need to take back the power of the "yes." Little girls should not be taught to always say "no," and little boys should not be taught that their manliness hinges on always saying, or getting, "yes." All genders should be taught how to know when they are truly ready to say "yes," and only then will we get back the power of "no."

So, it's not "men" as a general population that I should be afraid of, and it never has been. What my uncles, brothers, father, and cousins should have been teaching me my whole life was to fear and fight a society in which a) girls are continuously told their bodies are not theirs, and b) boys are continuously told to staunchly shun femininity, but relentlessly chase females. Even by women, and in every form of media, the female form is open to more scrutiny than anything else: more than the rampant corruption in our banks and politics, more than the completely avoidable, careless human practices that are raping our planet to the eventual point of our own extinction. Nothing is more carefully and systematically dissected, maintained, and regulated on every level of our society than the female form, and we are taught that we need to scrutinize our own bodies even on top of that. Imperfection is not an option, and the idea that you can do what you want with your own body is offensive and even selfish.

V

In my adult life, many people have told me on multiple occasions that I am "the most complicated person they know," that I'm "difficult", and "too much." I've been continuously told I'm an "anomaly," an "enigma." People constantly tell me they can't figure me out. I've never purposefully aimed for that perception, but in a sense that is exactly what I want, because that means my life's work has been a success. Mystery is sexy, sexy is mystery, and both are me in a nutshell.

But on another level, really I think people have "trouble" figuring me out because the world is an anomaly to me, and I can't figure it out. I can see how my outward confidence in most other areas of my life can clash with my inner confusion of what is right and normal in a sexual sense. But that is because up until now, nearly every one of my sexual interactions has been a paradox: I have been systematically trained throughout my entire life to fear all of the ways that men would try to use my body, yet either chastised for being too hard on my gentleman suitors or pitied for not dating at all. I have been told that I am sexually appealing unceasingly, in every way possible, and in every type of outfit, but then asked with disdain why I dress and act so sexually when I specifically decide to show off my curves. I have been groped, fondled, and had my confusion taken advantage of so many times that I consider that to be normal, only to have those same guys go and crow to their friends about their big score; they had, after all, beat me in the game. So this is how I seem to come off to people as if I have little insecurity, when in reality I am plagued by it. And I know I am not the only one.

But what I've finally learned is that despite what much of our society would have us believe, I do live in a place and time where I can actually control my own sexuality. My female body does not have to be submissive. Having control over my body and myself does not mean abstaining from sex, it means actually making all of my sexual decisions for myself, for my own reasons. As females we truly have to start being our real selves in the world; sometimes, or most times, we will have to aggressively be ourselves, because sometimes or most times ourselves are aggressively attacked just for being what they are. It's time for us to take sole ownership of our own bodies, and it's time for us to make things weird.

I'm writing this now for any young girls out there who are confused or scared like I have been, and still am: some people will try to hurt you, so you have to be on your toes. But protecting yourself does not mean suppressing your sexuality, it means taking control of it in any way that you feel fit. Your body is yours. Your brain is yours. Do not ever let anyone else make you feel like they have more of a right to either of those precious things than you do. You'll need to use both to navigate this world, and you need to remember that you are the goddamn Commander in Chief. Because I can't stand the thought of any more generations of girls in this country going through the needless turmoil that I went through and am still experiencing. I cannot express how deeply I feel the ache in every one of my bones from 27 years of worrying about how the world perceives my body, and I need to do my part to protect anyone else I can from that.

You cannot control how other people perceive you, but you can control how you move through the world. You can be sexy and smart. In fact, to any partner who is worth anything, smart is sexy. The body does not function without the brain, and someone figuring out the riddle of your beautiful brain should be the only key to your bodily VIP access (even if that riddle is simply, "What has two thumbs and wants to have sex with you?"). These days I've learned to walk sexy, talk sexy, dress sexy, dance sexy, and slice up my foes with a razor tongue. I do it all for me, and by extension, for the people who have earned their key. As women we need to create our own mantra, for our sake and for the sake of all of the men and women who will come after us: our bodies are ours and our sexualities are ours, and when we want to, we can, and should be, both sexy and sexual. That's just how women are, and we shouldn't have to help it. These are our bodies, and only we have the right to decide what to do with them. It's about time Fem Farmers became obsolete.

A Reminder by Kit Hunt - Acrylic on 8"x10" canvas, 2017.

# Post-Traumatic Stress Disorder on Pontiac Trail

I could close my eyes and remember
the peach fuzz on your upper lip and how your tongue swirled in my mouth
during a long kiss; I could remember
the length each one of your fingers, sharp knuckles and grips,
caressing the nape of my neck, but remembering
your passionate chokeholds, and how we mounted on my kitchen counters
and on the carpet does not replace the memory
of you penetrating me as I wept
I remember. I remember
the window ajar and the candlelight dim
your bedroom smelling of cinnamon
I remember. I remember
asking you to use a condom,
and as you assured me that you had a Durex in your top right drawer,
you penetrated me with such force —
I never consented to unprotected sex.
the room darkened, I remember
the warmth of my tears, on my cheeks and on my clavicles,
and my ignored whimpers,
but even if you had stopped to ask
if you had done something wrong, you would have not committed
this moment to your memory,
because rapists do not dwell like we do...
we drive on an endless amounts of pavement, and we remember
post-traumatic stress disorder on Pontiac Trail
Screaming, throwing my fits to the trees, remembering
winter's brutality, under full moons and on mild afternoons

I skid on black ice, hoping to find a quiet darkness
my passenger's seat always empty, because I kept this memory
to myself for six months and when I told my mother,
she stared at the floor, leaving me in silence
and for a second, I felt as if I would never be impenetrable again

- Megan Murphy

# Anxiety Disorder

Chronically
living in
flight,
fight,
and freeze.

- Lachrista Greco

Untitled by Sara De Melo Teixeira

# Shark Teeth

There's a dust bunny beneath my bed
that grins at me at night
when the moon drips silken saccharine
into the crook of my elbow,
pools cool flame down my lifeline.

I am    not afraid
        too afraid     of dust bunnies

flumming in the shadows
        teeth of bedsprings
        jagged creak when tongues of lint lick lips and
Tongues, I think, more terrifying than this
handful of ash swilting through my fingertips.

But ash reminds me of fire reminds me of
moonlight,
        nighttime silhouette
        and snap-second of silence.
                        There are moves in this dance that have me
doubled over
spying rabbits under maudlin covers –

I have never seen a matching comforter set
that wasn't covered in dust.

                - Kali Noel Dodez

# No, Not Ever Again

I'm eating an orange on the
Church bound G train
Looking at my feet
And seeing that black + white
Doesn't make gray, but yellow
Yellow like a bad food metaphor
In a tragic mulatta novel
And I use to think that because the men
Didn't holler at me, or make obscene remarks
That I wasn't pretty enough,
Fucked up, right?
The train wheels agonizes to a stop
I disembark from one borough to the other
Fingers are sticky now, lungs ache
From afternoon sun
I talk too loudly with big brass teeth
My skin gleans like dragon scales
Those teeth and those fingers are useful
Tell the men on the street to fuck off
But this fear lingers, its quiet dull rhythm
the only one I've known
My defenses soften to reveal rawness
Like meat of an orange
It makes me cross the street
It makes me just pass on/cross
Must avoid the insatiables
I'll cry if I let another one touch me
With my word-binding taking hold
No, not ever again.

- Jennifer Caroccio

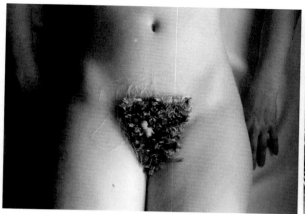

My Vagina by Vanessa Fleising - woven on hand-made loom, string, feather, toy baby, butterfly wing, 9" x 6" x 4", 2013.

My vagina represents my worries about pregnancy, my vagina as my ability to pop out babies, from vagina I came, my vagina as a soft cuddly place, my vagina as a place where dead butterflies live, my vagina as a place where butterflies fly freely, my vagina as a butterfly that has been trampled, my vagina as my soul, my vagina as something delicate that must not be taken advantage-of, my vagina as pleasure, my vagina that must be caressed softly like a feather, my vagina as a field of soft grass you can run in, my vagina as a field of soft grass you can lie-down and roll-around in, my vagina as color and beautiful, my vagina with light string coming out of it to protect itself whispering "no," but they are not heard nor seen, my vagina as delicate, my vagina as my troubles, my vagina as my heart and my love, my vagina as energy, my vagina as me.

# Ghosts

'Ere Dawn broke, and rosy-fingered
Stroked the sculpture of his face,
Lost was I in thoughts that lingered
In this dark and dismal space.

Time hath stained me with compassion
But I hardly can adore
How in a Plutonian fashion
Enter lost loves from before.

Enter Mem'ry, enter fellows,
O ye violents! O ye liars!
Midst the broken-bonèd bellows
Of my self-worth on the pyre!

Speak of nights I still abhor
Or raise thy sickly face to flame
That age-old wounds still scream in horror
At the mention of thy name!

Send me swimming in confusion
With your practiced honeyed-speech
Linking horror to illusion
That my youth you still can leech!

Lie to me now, screaming specters
That you earn your hateful keep!
Tears to alm you dream-infectors!
I cannot sleep! I cannot sleep!

- Kendalle Aubra

# Liefdesverdriet
# Alternative Title: Heartbreak (Hjärtesorg)

Allison Oaks

liefdesverdriet  */livdəsfərdrit/*

- (noun) an untranslatable Dutch word, *liefdesverdriet* expands on the meaning of heartbreak. It encompasses the full feelings of heartbreak, which includes the mental anguish one endures, but rarely speaks about. It holds the physical pain of depression, exhaustion, loss of appetite, insomnia, and overall sorrow. It is both the metaphorical and physical pain of the heart.

● ● ●

Afterwards, you won't laugh as much.
You won't even laugh the same way.
In fact, laughter often seems perverse, crude.
It invokes feelings of profound guilt.
How dare you be happy?
He's gone. Are you forgetting that?
How can you even smile in his absence?
You are forever scarred.

This night.
This night is burned into your consciousness forever.
It is a lovely September evening.
The breeze is cool and you can feel the slight chill of autumn biting in the air.

You open the windows in the nursery to clear the room after being closed up all day.

You lay him down, softly, sweetly.
You coo a bit together, sing softly.
He shows signs of tiredness, heavy eyes, but seems content.
He is calm, you are calm, you kiss him.
You set the music player to exhale soothing music.
You close the door gently and leave him to his peaceful interlude.

The past eight weeks has been hard on you.
A lot of ups and downs.
He was due on the 27th of July, but the doctors said he must come
out a week early.
He is a large baby growing within in your petite frame.
Not ideal.
You are induced, the pain is immense, but the birth itself is textbook.
He is healthy and strong.
He is born with thick black hair and deep, knowing eyes.
You see he is an old soul.
You hold him in your arms, you cry tears of happiness.
You name him Keir.

You shortly show signs of post-partum depression.
Your mood swings are relentless.
You cry, then scream, then cry more until you are empty.
Every feeling overwhelms you, the good and the bad.
Swinging from one extreme to the next.
Sleep is out of the question.
A new mother needing to feed your child recurrently, but the anxiety
leaves you cognizant.
Against your will you lay awake, yet you are relentlessly listless.
The paradox of motherhood.

As the weeks go by, your love blossoms.
You see the glint of recognition in his eyes.
You are his world, his everything.

A mother. His mother.
His head turns at the sound of your voice.
A gurgle uttered, meant just for you.
You sing with him and read him books, he smiles.
Your heart melts.

This night.
This night that will haunt you until you relinquish your life.
You walk in, the nursery is luxuriously cool.
But you stop.
You feel a tangible absence.
You look over into his crib.
You see him twisted unnaturally.
You cannot see his face.
You grab him, he is like ice.
You turn him, his face is blue, contorted in an unnatural grimace.
There is blood trickling from his lips.
Your heart knows, but your mind refuses.
This image sears itself into your memory, immutable.

You race down the hall, at a speed you didn't think yourself capable
of, to your telephone.
You call 911, the conversation is a blur.
Men are suddenly in your house.
They take you aside.
They are asking so many questions.
You just sit and stare.
*Is he allergic to any medications?*
*Does that mean he's alive?*
You feverishly grasp at straws.
They don't answer.
They look down as if ashamed to ask the question again.
They know it's futile.
*Is he allergic to any medications?*

*No.* You say.
Your mind both sees and does not see.
What is happening?

You drive to the hospital behind the ambulance.
You call your mother and just say *Go!*
You walk into the ER, it is almost empty.
The nurses look at you, is that pity in their eyes?
Yes, they know.
They meet you in the hallway and lead you directly to a private room.
You know what this means.
No. *No no no.*

You don't want to hear the words.
If they don't say it, it can't be true.
A nurse walks in, so solemn.
She whispers *I'm sorry.*
Oh god, it's true.
The world is suddenly dark.
You feel cold.
Completely numb.
*Do you want to see him?* They ask.
*You can go in, but you cannot touch him.*
You do want to see him, but you cannot move.
You cannot bring yourself to see your darling child covered in tubes, lifeless.
You fight with yourself, but cannot go.
Your mother goes in for you.
She tells you he is beautiful.
You cry.
For hours.
Days.
Weeks.

You hear phantom cries in the night.
You want to die.


Three days pass with no sleep.
You walk into the funeral parlor.
The smell of formaldehyde and old flowers is strong.
It makes your nostrils itch
*He's in the room down the hall.*
You follow them, unsure what you'll see.
Unsure if you want to see.
He is there, lying on a tray of sorts, dressed in his monkey pajamas, hooded with ears.
Your favourite outfit on him.
His skin looks waxen, lacking its natural glow.
He doesn't look like Keir.
He doesn't smell like Keir.
You hold him.
He is chilled, it feels so wrong.


For over an hour you stare at him, cry, hold his hand, caress his beautiful hair.
You stop, you feel something under the hood at the nape of his neck.
A careless, monstrous scar.
*Oh god.*
They performed an autopsy.
*Of course they did*, you think, but you don't want to feel the gruesome evidence.
They violated your beautiful child.
You cut locks of his hair, so you can have it with you always. *snip*
Each curl is perfect.
It's time.
You have to let him go.
You have to put him back on the tray.
You do so, gently, as is putting him down for a nap.

His mouth opens ever so slightly.
You gasp.
It pains you beyond words.
You leave crying, realizing this is the last time you will ever see him.
Tomorrow, he will be cremated.

You receive his ashes in a tiny box.
You feel a strange disassociation.
Surely, this vessel does not contain your child.
Absurd.
Your mother offers to give Keir her niche she bought for herself.
Right below your aunt, cater-corner to your grandparents.
There is a part of you that is glad he will be among family.
Part of you feels cheated.
He should be with you.
You put his heart-shaped urn within the niche.
You enclose a teddy bear made by you, with love.
You close the glass, and seal him in for eternity.
The finality is crushing.

Time moves forward against your will.
You want time to stop.
You want the world to mourn with you.
How can people go on with their lives as if nothing has happened?
He was here!
He was alive!
He was mine!
The weight of losing him slowly destroys you, your marriage, your job, your life.
You are a shell of your former self.
You try to bury it.
You MUST to survive.
But the pain refuses to be interred.

You divorce from Keir's father.

It is messy.

He grieves separately from you and he becomes toxic.

He tells you, *Get over it.*

As if it was nothing of consequence.

You know he is suffering in his own way.

You cannot help him, and he cannot help you.

It's over.

Your family helps you recover.

They are unwavering in their support.

You are grateful.

You and your mother lean of each other for support.

Without her, you're not sure if you'd still be alive.

Two pained women, strengthened by their love.

Years pass.

Six to be exact.

His birthdays come and go.

You suffer every year.

Sometimes more.

Sometimes less.

It floods over you.

Everything is gray.

The world seems hopelessly bleak.

You lose large fragments of time to melancholia.

*Where does it go?* You often wonder.

He still haunts you to this day.

The images still as clear as the day they were forged, harsh and unyielding.

It hurts you every day, the absence of him.

You hope that one day you'll find peace.


Keir Liam Oaks 2009/07/22 - 2009/09/16
I love you.
Written 2015/10/23

Bath Woman by Vanessa Fleising - acrylic paint and human hair on canvas mounted on 34.5'' x 57'' wood panel, 2011.

# XV – Coda –

Why do you wear these scars?

Because the devil touched me

And I lived to tell the tale.


- Rebecca Hilgraves

# Little Volcanoes

You
are
the
lifelong reminder
of what he did to
me.

And

for
my
survival,
I must choose
to love you.

- Lachrista Greco

# Acidity

today you are the twist in my gut like knives

and I am choking on mint gum and cold water

and I am tired of thinking of you.


- Kali Noel Dodez

# Some days are harder than others

They tell me just stop thinking about it
As I can just flip a switch
As if it's always that simple

They tell me to think about something else
But how can I focus on the future
When the past won't leave me alone?

And I don't know how to explain it
When I've always been the listener
And never put my problems on others
I don't know how to explain it
Because I've never tried

And now I'm slowly pulling away
From my loved ones because
I don't want them to worry over me
The way I worry over them

People say a perfect memory is a gift
But not for me
When I can remember the screaming
As clear as if I'm back in that room again
And unable to do anything

And I swore when I left
I swore an oath
That I would never feel that helpless again

Some days are harder than others
When I can still see the blood

And have to look at my hands, white and clean
To know that I'm not back there anymore

I can't watch certain movies anymore
Those scenes intermingle
 And leave me curled on the floor
Shuddering and sobbing like a child

I thought it was all in my head
Maybe I'm as crazy as I claim to be
But whatever it is or isn't
It's real
And I'm real
And I'm here
And I am now
And I am alive.

- Oksana Keeney

# The Old Self Laid to Rest

Kit Hunt

I have learned that sharing personal stories is important.

It is empowering for people to read accounts of survival. It is important for people to share their stories. For all we know, there is an isolated person out there, with no hope at all, who will come across your story and be moved enough to take action or be comforted. It can save lives. Reading the stories of other people has saved my own life, and kept me going. It makes me feel less alone in this.

Most of those like myself that have experienced horrific childhood trauma, domestic violence, assault, or rape are silenced for a great deal of time about our experiences, in addition to shutting those memories away for survival and not wanting to engage in sharing them with themselves or others out of fear. Sometimes the memories are shut away somewhere in our brains to protect us until they really start to hurt us. It is what chronic, long term trauma has conditioned us to do. Once told, our stories can be powerful and life changing. My own healing depends on everything coming out of the dark, and being completely honest about how painful that experience was. Dissociation is a survival tactic that can only last for so long: my actual survival has been at stake because as a former victim, I simply could not bear to even talk about any of my trauma with anyone.

I guess you could say when I was born, I didn't have a chance to have a "normal" childhood. I was surrounded by generations of dysfunction on both my mother's side and my father's side of the family. My parents married right out of high school. My dad is a college graduate and my mother has a high school education. She tried to go to college at 19, but my father blocked her way out the door, said "where do you think you're fucking going?" and told her he would kill her if she stepped out that door to get an education. When I was still in grade school, my father beat my mother behind closed doors, and soon was bold enough to hit her really hard on the left side of her head at his company picnic. They made up this elaborate lie about how it happened. My mother was crying at the picnic table, holding her face. She permanently lost all hearing in her left ear.

Once I determined that my innocent child like behavior enraged my father and annoyed my mother, to keep myself safe I became a quiet, withdrawn child and obedient to a fault. I "protected" myself by staying in my room a lot, locking the door, and playing fantasy role plays with dolls, horses, and matchbox cars that could take me out of the house I was living in. I had a few friends but I couldn't relate to them...my life was so dark and disturbing because of my parents and I could not really be me. I counted the days until I could grow up as fast as possible and escape. I remember telling my mother that I wished I was an adult so I could leave and be free. I was 10.

My great grandmother was mentally ill. She ran away from the Appalachian Mountains and left my grandmother, who she had conceived with a married sailor, in some asylum/home until she wandered back from wherever she had been for years. Over the years, she changed her name 6 times and lived out of a whisky bottle. Her daughter, my grandmother Lucille "was crazy", according to extended family, and was put in a psych ward several times when my mother was a kid. When I was in grade school, Lucille left the family once again, didn't remember why, and was taken back home and given medication to make her more "sedate." No one in the family dared discuss these matters when I was young. I found these things out when I was an adult and conducting family research. I was not allowed to see my grandparents for almost 5 years before I started high school. My mother wasn't speaking to them, so my brother and I had to do the same thing. All of a sudden, they were just gone. No more Sunday dinners or talks on the phone I used to love. Just like my dog my dad used to beat in front of me, almost every week. She was just gone one day, too. My parents told me "she had gone to a farm where she can be happy and run free." I knew my dad had beat my dog to death and it was all a lie. It made me even more afraid of the house I lived in.

My mother started showing signs of mental illness when I was very young, and my father took on the role of his abusive, violent parents. The physical violence, verbal abuse, and isolation started when I was just a baby. When my mother chooses to share a childhood memory with me, it is "remember that time your father threw you out the window, and told me he would fucking kill me if I helped you?" At the holiday party last December, my father entertained a table of party guests with a story about how he tried to have me arrested when I was 15 years old. He was laughing hysterically but the other guests responded with awkward silence. "She was only 15, Dave," my Aunt sheepishly commented. He said he didn't care.

My brother and I were severely beaten on a weekly basis starting when I was 3 years old. I was beaten the worst because I kept peeing in my underwear almost every day starting at age 3. No one took me to the doctor or sat me down and asked me what I thought was going on. I could have articulated that if asked. Both of them told me that I was "lazy" "undisciplined" "disgusting" and beat me for it. I was terrified every day. I was also locked in my bedroom for months at a time as punishment, only allowed to leave for meals and school. I was often stripped of my clothes when I was hit with various items. It always left bruises. My mother refused to wash my underwear, and instead told me I would have to wear diapers. By age 4, I guess they couldn't stand it anymore and finally took me to a doctor, who diagnosed me as having a malformed internal urethral sphincter and ordered surgery right away. My parents have never apologized for this, and have said things like "well, we were just doing our best!" A poor, programmed excuse for anything. I have my parents to thank for cultivating the deep roots that led to a life of personality disorders, a dysfunctional filter and trauma.

My official diagnosis as of today: Complex Post Traumatic Stress Disorder, Generalized Anxiety Disorder, Depersonalization Disorder and Obsessive Compulsive Disorder. I am currently taking 3 different kinds of psych meds, and will probably be on those for the rest of my life. Since 2003, when I got diagnosed with PTSD, doctors have tried six different kinds of medications to treat my illness, as we just haven't gotten them quite right yet. Often, I am frustrated viewing the world through my illness and re-learning to communicate with the world in a healthy way. I work full time, I'm an artist, I am a mother, a community activist, and I keep going because I do know that recovery is a process, and I often compare it to doing a long hike. I'm a hiker that has climbed 2 mountains and done many trails. When my mind makes things unbearable during flare ups, I imagine I am on the trail, backpack on, and ready to cross that really challenging spot in the hike. I know I'll get there.

Society knows about PTSD mainly from what we see in the media. We get the impression that PTSD is something that only war vets come home with. Go online and most PTSD information is about combat exposure in the military. Treating war veterans is extremely important, yes. However: women who haven't served in the military, who need PTSD treatment due to domestic violence, rape, and other trauma do not have many resources online or otherwise and often go without any kind of treatment or medication. Speaking from experience, having PTSD has a huge negative impact on socioeconomic status. The symptoms interfere with work, relationships, and just about everything else in daily life. Women seem to be the forgotten warriors in the battle for everyday survival in trying to live with PTSD and other co-occurring disorders. Support groups and help are difficult to find if you are a woman with PTSD. Most doctors do not specialize in treating this. There aren't enough therapists that are trained in helping clients with PTSD. Medication is expensive, mostly trial and error, and not something that you can take alone without therapy to go along with it. Having PTSD requires an intricate, consistent network of support. 10 out of 100 women will develop PTSD in their lifetime; 4 out 10 men will; yet most of the studies and information about treatment we have about PTSD has come from men serving in Vietnam and other combat zones. Women need their own voice, specialized treatment, and support system so we can start to see progress and healing.

My own journey to PTSD was a long one. That horrific abuse endured when I was child through my teens; almost raped at 12, raped at 15 years old, and raped again at 20; a trusted boyfriend who physically injured my spine when I was 19 years old so severely that my vertebrae was dislodged, resulting in the loss of 2 discs. Having never dealt with any of the previous trauma I had endured, my mind started unraveling in my 30's, right around when I started college, was working a lot, and dealing with new stressors. I was put on anti-anxiety medication for the first time in my life. I went to therapy. I was married to a guy that would call me "crazy" or ignore me when my symptoms acted up. My anxiety disorder was not something to be discussed, ever. I decided it would be better not to show anyone the pain I was going through, act perfect, and just concentrate on college and raising my kid. This allowed me to take every single bad thing that had happened to me and compartmentalize it and put everything away for what I thought was forever in order to concentrate on more "positive" things. Life was going to be good again, I decided, and I would put the past behind me. I did not take another pill. That was in 2003.

Yes. I "put the past behind me" for more than 20 years, which I now know is just some old saying that does not mean shit to someone who has had my experiences. The "past" of unresolved trauma came roaring back with gnashing teeth in 2010 when I went through a terrible divorce that left me homeless, jobless, penniless and entangled in a judicial system completely comprised of men that had no sympathy for a woman like me. I went to social services and begged to see a psychiatrist and get some medication, because I feared for my safety. No, they said, it will be a month before someone can see you. Goodbye. I went without medication or counseling for almost 3 more years, because I did not have money, health insurance or a doctor. Finally, in 2013, I was almost killed in an automobile accident. More damage to my spine and bone fragments in my neck. I couldn't work for 4 months. My car was totaled. I ran out of money. I could not function, and my mind finally snapped. I felt like I had lost everything all over again, after working so hard to get back on my feet in 2010. All I felt was pain and fear every second of the day. The ground had finally dropped out from under me, and I did not know that I would slowly lose my mind that summer and into the next year. Every single bit of unresolved trauma from the last 40 years had resurfaced due to the accident, and my ability to compartmentalize any of that like I usually could was gone, replaced with visceral, physical, debilitating symptoms. I didn't have money for mental health services; I hobbled into an urgent care, spent my last $100 and found a doctor that prescribed an anti-anxiety medication that I am still taking. I will always remember his kindness and ability to see what I needed in that moment. My treatment for PTSD had begun, albeit with tiny little steps.

I wrote about my experiences with it a lot that year:

*"Well, you LOOK fine." Ignorant fucking assholes.*

*My neck is bad. It feels like it has shards of glass in it. I cannot look up, down or sideways. It hurts all the time. My back is messed up once again. I hurt my leg when the car rolled.*

*I know…at least I am alive, right?*

*I am now on several pain relieving drugs, as well as panic attack meds. The accident has opened up all sorts of doors to panic and anxiety once again. I can't really eat or sleep. Dreams and thoughts of the accident pervade my waking and sleeping life. I am weepy. I feel alone.*

*I am back on my required dose of medication after 3 days and the terrible, debilitating blackness has lifted. I forgot to take almost 6 doses last week, which is substantial. It affected me greatly, though it wasn't until the fifth day or so that I started noticing and I felt like my mind was unraveling with runaway thought.*

*I do not wish this on anyone. Anxiety disorders are terrible. If you haven't experienced this on a daily basis and struggled through even the most simple of days, it's difficult to explain to you.*

Flash forward to the present.

I have made a lot of progress since that trip to the urgent care. I am taking my prescribed medication everyday despite the side effects. I am seeing a doctor regularly to talk about symptoms, adjusting medications. I am keeping track of my moods every day. I like my little green pill box. I go to work every day and do the best I can even when my mind is screaming no. I work on finishing my college degree. I constantly read about PTSD and talk openly now with others about it. I couldn't do that before, so that is a huge step in my recovery. I am not isolating myself even on the days I feel like it. I am reaching out to my friends if I am having a really bad day. I am talking about my mental illness with my brother, who shared many years of hardship with me. I am setting limits. I am creating boundaries. I am practicing self- care. I am learning to cry after spending many years not being able to do that. I am letting go of perfection. I have excluded all toxic people, which includes my parents and people I have known for decades I am letting go of the shame I felt when I was told I was mentally ill. I am proud of my wounds, my scars, and my pain. And if you are reading this and feeling your wounds, I am proud of you. Keep Going.

Disassociate by Christine Lane, 2015.

# To my witches with OCD

have you ever wondered what someone could do
with the sadness crystallized in your tears after they distill away
into the lining of your therapist's wastepaper basket?

is there a moment when the world of spells drops away
to reveal an animal void screaming: 'NOW!'
a changeling in the place of your moon-smooth worship?

do you fear the moments when you can still feel
his hands on your body, torso
a psychosomatic cauldron, crotch locked tight
in the post-mortem chastity belt of your rape recollection?

have you ever worshipped to the fact that all your cells have fully
regenerated

since the last time he touched you have you ever cried so hard

you thought you could reverse the past have you ever burned your
ouija board

to prevent fear from coming after you have you ever shredded letters
you wrote

because the truth was too real have you ever washed the skin off
your hands prayerfully

have you ever tried to exorcise something that couldn't possibly have
happened to you

have you ever written a chapbook about the baby you lost and then
left it in a stranger's library

have you ever shared a room with your own ghost?

have you ever wondered if it was practicing a belief in magic that made you crazy?

more so than anything else?

than any of this ever could, or will?

I have.

it has taken everything in me to decide when to separate the ritual from my compulsion. I still want to run back screaming for my grief, to gather the bale of my diamond-shaped tears

and steal them back from my confessional room.

> \-    Lago Lucio

# I wish I were the moon

Serenity, tranquility,

Femininity.

I wish I could look down

Upon this earth

From far enough to see

Beauty.

If I had fit that mould

Ethereal, ephemeral,

The luna venus

Observed but never heard

Perhaps I would have stayed

A statue

Stared at but never touched.

My arms, my head are missing.

I see nothing

Wrap my arms around nothing

Say nothing

Sing nothing

But the parts all touched

When the warden wasn't looking

Are still there

Still under your gaze

When all the parts of me that mattered

Are broken off.

If I had been a better statue,

Maybe the warden would have

Nothing.


Now I am not a statue.

I am a lesson.

I am the 'or else'

Your mother learned to put

On the end of her warnings,

Make sure he rapes the other girl.

Unsaid, but heard

It is written on the moon

On the inside of your maxi pad

On the tags of your lingerie

By where it says 'seduce your man'

With three exclamation marks

And the promise of sex without orgasms

Making sure your tummy is flat.

I am the other girl.

I am the girl who didn't wear the rape

Preventing fingernail polish

And now fathers load their daughters

Onto my podium

And tell them I'm what happens

When

When anything.

- Evie Wolfe

# I do not like the color purple.

I'm better off alone.
Weak coffee isn't exactly "plans," but
I prefer the company of books
to that of broken bones.

I do not like the color purple.
He stumbles in violet.
What's not to trust in bourbon breath?
What color are these glasses?

I do not like the color purple.
Bed frames can look like graves.
A hand around your throat really is
Forced perspective.

I do not like the little things.
Blood's aftertaste is bitter.
Please listen when I tell you,
"I do not like the color purple."

- Laurel Posakony

Silent Killer: Domestic Violence Survivor Tribute by Jess Safely - watercolor on watercolor paper, 2016

# Anatomy of Acceptance

N.J.

I was twenty-three years old when I was diagnosed with Post-Traumatic Stress Disorder.

It was a sunny Saturday afternoon in the spring and I was feeling drained from the workweek. I sat in the dimly lit office with The Therapist, a tall and lean brown-skinned woman with an ageless face and soothing voice, trying to answer a single question she had asked me. She was not writing much in the yellow notepad on her lap; instead she was staring directly at me, nodding her head as I ran off with my emotions and talked in circles. At some point, she handed me some tissues with a reassuring smile as I choked on my words for forty minutes.

I timidly decided to talk to someone because of how out of control my life was beginning to feel. I had learned about mental disorders for the first time as in teen, where I was forced to talk to someone for a suspected anxiety disorder in high school. Confused, I told my mother and she immediately put a stop to it, assuring the school that I was fine and would make it to college, which I of course did. During my freshman year, I experienced a couple of heavy incidents and was pushed by those who knew to speak to a councilor on campus. That didn't really work out. I was uncomfortable divulging my life to a stranger, especially one who was nodding off as I was confessing my pain.

Now here I was four years later trying, for the last time, to make sense of everything.

I finally calmed down enough to stop talking. The Therapist waited a few moments and smiled. She gently noted that she saw anxiety and depression, which I was not surprised about. I wasn't a fan of the labels, but I did come into our first couple of sessions sobbing about my recent struggles to get out of bed and my lack of interest in eating – a pattern I was beginning to notice in myself that would last for long stretches at a time for seemingly no reason. But then, The Therapist kept talking. She mentioned something about "severe traumas." She strung along a few more sentences and all I could remember hearing was, "Post-Traumatic Stress Disorder." I furrowed my brows in confusion but she didn't seem phased; The Therapist continued talking while still looking straight into my eyes. She said that she had to ask me if I wanted medication to manage myself for a little while and I waved her off, still trying to process what she was telling me. She scheduled another session; I paid my $40 co-pay and left her office in a hurry.

With the number 7 train roaring above me, I took the loneliest walk down Queens Boulevard trying to convince myself that The Therapist was wrong. I had never been a soldier or lived in a country where I had to worry about flying robots killing me. *I'm probably just too wrapped up in my feelings again*, I thought. I was embarrassed that I had unloaded on her so quickly and thought maybe her conclusion was based on my being too dramatic. I thought about how I was always told I was too sensitive as a kid and my cousins telling me to "act regular" if they thought I was in a funk. My father would always demand to know why I appeared to be deep in thought at the table as I scarfed down Rice-A-Roni meals in silence on weekend visits back home with him in East New York. I didn't think anyone wanted me to be sad, and certainly no one would want me to have PTSD.

I reached the apartment I was sharing with my then-fiancé-now-husband, sat down and suddenly burst into tears. How could I be so sad and broken? I thought I could be the strong person everyone said I was meant to be. I had learned not to cry in public, to never let people know what I was thinking and to move on from unfortunate things that may have happened – or so I thought. I didn't think my accomplishments thus far were too shabby. Statistically, being a poor child of color born to teenage and divorced parents seemed to doom me to failure. I didn't go to an Ivy League but with my public college education and very little student debt, I snagged a decent job related to my field during the Great Recession. I could afford rent in my post-college apartment in a charming neighborhood in Queens, which was just a short train ride to Manhattan. I knew how to save money and still enjoy a Netflix and Hulu subscription without cable. I expected to be able to handle problems because I had no time to crumble up and feel hopeless but there I was, Miss Accomplished, crying for the umpteenth time in my brightly lit living room knowing that my grandmothers, aunts, cousins and even my mother had dealt with far more challenges than I did. Being told I was sick made me feel like the biggest failure to everyone who knew me.

I ultimately decided not to skip my next session and went back to see The Therapist three times a week in both her Manhattan and Queens offices. At first, I thought it would be a good way to make things normal quickly and quietly – whatever that would mean for me – but as I slowly began to accept my diagnosis I decided to not put a deadline on the journey. In the beginning, I was secretive about why I couldn't always join a happy hour or wasn't up for hanging out on the weekends. I was consumed with the fear of anyone finding out that I had to talk to someone in order to keep sane. I thought I hid everything well at work because I still showed up and did what I needed to do, but knew if co-workers looked at me too closely they might see the cracks. I was having issues with my then-fiancé-now-husband at the time, and was afraid that we would be completely done once he learned that I was a confirmed "nutcase."

I spent countless hours online searching for black girls like me, who were timidly admitting that they struggled with finding help and acceptance because we weren't "those kind of people." Weakness and emotions I had learned were for White girls who could afford to have their feelings coddled. I remembered a college theater class I took while in my junior year of high school, where a White girl recovering from an eating disorder told me that her disease was selfish, since she was always in the hospital disrupting everyone's lives. And even though we read Ntozake Shange's <u>For Colored Girls Who Have Considered Suicide/When the rainbow is Enuf</u>, I knew there was no room for any of that in my family. I had to get good grades and take care of my siblings whether I felt good or not. My cues from television, where black girls were often the cool, sassy sidekicks, had everything under control. They loved their body shape, took care of everyone and loved only black men. I knew I struggled with this notion because as a teen, my mother learned that I was a cutter and told me I was acting like a White girl and Nana wondered aloud why I would do such a thing. When an uncle I was close to was murdered, I remember as a child searching my great-grandmother's face for tears and couldn't even find sadness; somehow I knew I was supposed to be like that.

I didn't want my friends to know I was struggling and I most certainly didn't want to reveal it to my family. As time went on, I blurted it out to a few people anyway, because I realized most of my life had been about keeping secrets and I was too tired to do that anymore, even if it did make me look unstable and weak. My fiancé-now-husband took my diagnosis fairly well and it actually helped bring our relationship to a better place. The friends who knew were surprised but were extremely supportive and understanding; one of my younger sisters who was in college emailed me any helpful articles she could find and asked me questions, so I became comfortable talking to her as well.

I managed to tell my father over the phone one evening after avoiding his calls for a little while. He shocked me when he immediately addressed it and assured me that it was okay and even revealed that his own mother had a mental illness – something I never knew. I started answering his phone calls more often and he always make an asked how I was progressing with therapy. I still felt some shame with what I thought was a huge unaddressed problem: being mentally ill and Black. Because of this, I could not see myself in my paternal grandma as she was not black and I still struggled with the notion of being too open about my illness.

Eventually, I mustered up the courage to tell Nana. I was prepared to explain to her, with evidence, that sometimes black girls feel sad too and that PTSD wasn't just for soldiers but it turned out there was no need. She questioned what could have caused it but she quickly became my number one supporter, even coming up with the notion of a "toolbox," used to help me cope with my issues that The Therapist readily incorporated into our sessions. In the almost two years I spent being treated with psychotherapy, I learned that my unexplained, random chest pains and breathing problems that I started having at around thirteen were anxiety attacks, that my self-starvation was anorexia, and my seemingly out-of-no-where nausea at the smell of original-scented dishwashing soap was something called a "trigger" for my PTSD. It was also helpful that The Therapist was not only a woman of color, but specialized in treating trauma in minorities, which was completely coincidental since I chose someone at random through my insurance.

I was scared that I wouldn't know who I was once I learned to manage my symptoms, but these days I can tell when something is "off" because the old feelings I once felt all the time are now alien. I finally know what "regular" could be like for me. There are still times in my everyday life where I curl up and cry and need a few days to recover, but I am fortunate enough to have a great support system. I don't view my illness as make believe or selfish because like someone with the flu, I can't help being sick. Sometimes I need to be taken care of and my husband, family and friends are happy to do so, even though I know they don't fully understand.

I'm okay with being black, a woman and a little sick; and others, whether they are women of color or not, should know that it's okay for them too.

# black girl.

dark skin, kinky topped woman..
the oppressed species.
love thy woman, love thy self.
embrace your shade
love your locks.
weak minds will try and break you.
kill them with confidence
and you
will
thrive.

- A'yonna Titus

# A Week in the Life of a Southern Queer
# 6.13.16

Saturday.
I organized my office's participation in our local gay pride parade
where I was greeted at the entrance with a larger-than-life protest
sign that read,

"Got
Aids
Yet?"

with some twisted bible verse
stamped below it
as some mark of credible proof that our existence is sinful.

Thursday.
I walked the person I'm dating to the airport security check.
I anxiously hugged her
and made it quick
because the airport wasn't that crowded
and we were afraid to draw attention to ourselves.
Despite not knowing when I'll get to see her again,
we didn't kiss goodbye
Because it's still Oklahoma,
And it's safer if we pass as straight.

Sunday.
I woke up early to the news
of the mass slaughter of 50 innocent queer people.
I spent the day crying and educating,
in between trips to the grocery store and the gym
because life will go on tomorrow without us.

The world
doesn't stop turning
when more queer people lose their lives.

The world
Barely pauses to critique how we grieve.
Oblivious
to the pain that we feel in our bones
because that could have been us.
Our loved ones.
Our families.
Our families who chose us regardless of who we love
While our birth families shunned us.

Monday.
Our grief spills over.

- Darci McFarland

# —A List of Times People *Almost* Invaded My Body and I Didn't Stop Them—

Haley Myers-Brannon

My feet were cold but my knees were burning because the heater blew so hot.

The van I learned to drive in, the man who told me to view potholes in the road as children so we would avoid them-Neglecting to teach us that a swerving vehicle is much more dangerous than tire damage. There is so much to say about this that I've avoided telling the stories entirely, but here are some things:

1. I watched a movie where a girl seduced a married man. She was 14 but pretended to be 20 and I identified with her. I found her intriguing, encompassing, like ivy on a house. Also, this familiarized me with shame.

2. I was 14. Maybe 13. I was so horny all of the time. I would grind against chairs under me. Imagine myself in compromising positions with compromising individuals. Constant shameful thoughts.

3. I made a joke to him about sex in the back of the van. Or something. I honestly don't remember the conversation. I do remember him saying he would pull off into the woods. I do remember the pot brownies. I remember later, talking to an attorney or a judge or some man in a suit trying to be gentle with adult words lying and saying I didn't know they were pot brownies. More shame.

4. I remember imagining the woods. Dirty, adult, secret sex with my best friends' 50 something year old dad and thinking how much like that girl in the movie I would be. I remember telling him no-changing my mind at the woods' entrance and laughing it off like I'd

been joking the entire time. Being so scared, so ashamed of being scared.

5. My best friend and I later that day walked to the Mexican restaurant down the road by ourselves- high. So high. Laughing. Clinging to autonomy like an oxygen mask at high altitude- it belonged to us. How guarded I was of my secret with her father. How ashamed I was.

6. We started a fight with a group of 6 or so 19-20 year old girls. Spewed every hateful and combative word we knew at them. Who the fuck knows why. Maybe we wanted our toughness to be tangible. Maybe, somewhere inside of me, I wanted to prove that I could protect myself, that I could guard my own castle. They crossed the street and we stood motionless as they approached us. We wouldn't stop screaming at them. Carved our voices into razorblades. One girl grabbed my arm and said, "You're so young. You shouldn't be here. You need to be more careful."
That was the second time in one day that someone whom I had invited to touch me, didn't, and I felt waves of relief and shame wash over me.

7. I no longer remember if I went to court for it or if I just gave them a letter to read. I have re-written days of this story so many times in order to view it from every angle that I have forgotten some things. I know that this is where I picked up shame like a second language. Where I learned that if something *almost* happens to you- no matter if it unravels you like a spool of thread- you do not get to live like you're affected by it. You get to be reminded of how lucky you are- that when you ran away, he didn't chase you- that he only ever called to taunt you after that night, he never came by- that he told all your friends about it, which incriminated him so you didn't have to face as rough of a court proceeding. So what that it was the summer before high school, so what that he told all of your young friends that

73

you "wanted it, begged for it". So what they called you names. Nothing \*happened\* to you. You will be reminded as an adult, when you call your parent to tell her how proud you are of yourself for telling your serious boyfriend about this incident, and she will say, "Which version did you tell him? That he actually hurt you, or the truth?" and in the tower of adulthood, you will feel so small.

8. His daughter, my best friend, was in the shower. He came in and beckoned me quietly out of the room. He walked into his bedroom and behind me shut and locked the door. Secret shame. To this day I don't voice my discomfort to closed and locked doors for the same reason I didn't back then. Because I can protect myself. Because, like my dad told me at the age of 6 when he wrestled me and I cried, "Don't get yourself into situations you can't handle- nobody wants to play with a girl who cries." I never cry. Everyone wants to play with me.

9. He told me to sit on his lap and move around. It was just like sitting on the chairs. I was just like the girl. I didn't even have to lie about my age. My hands were shaking so badly I wished I could sit on them. I stared at the door from his lap. I said 'No' as I stood up, – I was ashamed but I laughed like I had been joking the entire time and I walked, slowly, to the door- because running would imply I had gotten myself into a situation I couldn't handle. He grabbed my arm and begged me to stay. Called me a tease. A term I abhor but polish like a trophy to this day.

We are forever learning and unlearning the balance of power.

10. I was 22 when I finally read something that unlocked me. Lauren Brazzle was reading one of her poems and she said, "For years I thought I was a slut. At some point, slut became a cool thing to be. Older men always liked me because I was so mature. I still polish

---

74

that trophy… I hate when people talk about their abuse. It wasn't even abuse. I was just a slut. I don't need to talk about it."

11. When I was 19, I met a law student who invited me over late at night after I told him I was a virgin and I didn't have a car. He picked me up in a BMW and was drinking Whiskey out of a Camelbak water bottle. The doors on his car locked automatically and my feet were cold but my knees were burning. He had a full bar in his house. He kissed me hard on the mouth and got on top of me and I reminded him, "No, No" and he said, "It's okay, It's okay?" a question and a statement at once, an assertive formality of consent; A contract I couldn't read. I said, "Yes" because I don't get myself into situations I can't handle. Because people don't play with girls who cry. He pulled his pants off and I subtly laughed and said I changed my mind and I walked, not ran, to his front door, where he grabbed my arm and said, "I didn't hold you down. You're being a tease."

I called my roommate and waited for her on the street a block away. That night I told my roommate what happened; I asked her "am I allowed to feel so undone by this?" and she said "You're lucky. He didn't chase after you." I saved him in my phone as "Ryan (ruined my summer)" and I took to neatly wrapping the thread around the spool again.

12. When I was 17 I wrote him a letter. I had found his mug-shot and was filled with guilt, as heavy as cement, when I found out he had lost his house and lived in a van after he was released from jail. I felt shame at getting myself into a situation I couldn't handle and for it ruining his life. I said, "Please know that I don't hate you. I had a dream I saw you in heaven. I'm sorry for ruining your life." and I fucking sent it.

We are forever learning and unlearning the balance of power.

I don't spill out like I used to. I lived for years with a "For Lease"
sign in my ribcage hoping a tenant would come along and treat the
moldy floors. Rip everything up and build something new to stand
on. If I wrote him a letter today, it would say, "You are a piece of
shit. I am sorry that you felt in your gut that it was okay to claim a
13 year old's body as property. I am sorry that because she got away
and you did not chase her that you felt as though you had done
nothing wrong. Because of you she learned how complex and
layered the word, "No" can be; that it only stops the action at hand
but the effects continue for a long while after. You are a piece of
shit, but also I hope that someone loves you enough to not leave you
alone in this world."

I don't know how to write something I don't plan to read in public.
Here I hand a key to every pair of ears gathered in front of me and I
say, "Go ahead. Open me up."
I don't spill out like I used to. Just the occasional leaky roof,
dripping faucet. No more flooded bathrooms.

No molded floor.

# Running

## Victoria Grovich

"When the ride stops, we're gonna run, okay?" my girlfriend tells me.

We're at the state fair, on our second ride of the night, and one of my trigger songs has just come on.

"I knew this was going to happen," I say.

"Me too."

Not that it would be a hard thing to predict. My trigger songs are all from the same band. They're popular and play almost constantly. I never know when I'll hear them next. I never know when I'll next be hiding in the bathroom or running out of a store. Even just asking someone to change a song on the radio can get so tedious after a while. But if I don't, there's no telling how I'll react. I might be mildly triggered for a few moments or need days afterwards to recover. I might suffer silently or have a full-blown panic attack. There's really no telling.

The ride stops, the bar unlocks, and my girlfriend grabs my hand. People are probably giving us looks and wondering why we're in such a rush to get out. They probably think we're rude. But we're not thinking about them right now. We're focused on running.

I'm so tired of running.

. . .

I like to think that I lost my virginity when I was seventeen, but really, I don't know. She started touching me when I was maybe three or four or five. I don't quite remember. I also don't remember how old I was when it stopped. I didn't hear much about child on child sexual assault until I was older, and I still don't know what constitutes as girl on girl rape. I grew up thinking that what happened to me was irrelevant, that it didn't count.

I was uncomfortable and awkward with touch when I was younger. When I learned about STIs (then known as STDs), I was terrified I might have one. I completely rejected my sexuality. The only knowledge I had of girls being together was her, and that wasn't right. It made me sick. Even after the abuse stopped, she remained in my life for many years. The older I got, the more I craved her approval, and that made me sick too.

At sixteen, I could no longer ignore my sexuality. I was gay, I liked girls, and I hated myself for it. She made me sick, and instead of those sick feelings staying with her where they belonged, they crept into my love life and contaminated it completely. *Girls don't like girls. This is wrong. You can't be with girls. It's like being with* her. *You know that was wrong. How is being gay any different?*

It destroyed me.

Later that same year, my friend and I went to the park one night. We were hoping to find drugs, but we wanted them for different reasons. She wanted a good time. I wanted to get high enough to escape. There was torture in my head, and some part of me thought I could erase it. Get high. Hook up. Prove once and for all that either I could make myself stop liking girls--and like boys instead--or I couldn't.

I didn't know it then, but the stakes were as high as I was, and I was really, really high. I couldn't keep my eyes open, and I forgot my own name. The higher I got, the more realization set in: I didn't like boys. Not when I was sober and not when I was so high off my ass that my thoughts were barely my own. We were with maybe six or seven guys, and I couldn't find remote interest in a single one. In fact, my friend is the only one who became even slightly interesting to me in that state. I liked her hair. I liked her body. I liked when she joked about us getting drunk and hooking up. And I realized I was stuck. I liked girls. No amount of drugs or alcohol was going to change that. I felt defeated and ashamed of myself.

Then things got a little worse. We didn't know the guys we got high with. We hadn't cared. He kept telling me to take more, and I did. He himself barely had any, and the other guys did the same. I was so high, I could barely tell up from down, and he molested me. My friend watched.

After that night, my life changed drastically, and I began suffering from what I now know as PTSD. The first week I was constantly panicked and near tears. I wore baggy t-shirts and no make-up in contrast to my usual thick eyeliner and tight tank tops. I fell back into my eating disorder and self-harm. I couldn't stop thinking about killing myself.

As the months went on, I kept waiting for it to just go away, but it didn't. I continued having panic attacks and breakdowns. It seemed like the most trivial things could trigger me into being zoned out all day or crying my eyes out the entire night. I was irritable and argued over stupid things. It wasn't so much about the arguments themselves as it was needing to gain back some control. I was afraid of the dark. I couldn't stand touch, whether it was someone I didn't know accidentally brushing against me or someone I did know giving me a hug. It didn't matter. My touch issues isolated me, and they made me miserable.

As winter crept in, I was still having breakdowns almost every night. My depression and anxiety were getting worse. I was suicidal again, but this time it was different. I didn't *want* to die. I didn't *want* to kill myself. I wanted to live. I wanted to love my new girlfriend fearlessly. I wanted to go out with friends. I wanted to spend time with my family. I wanted to make the most out of my senior year of high school and plan for whatever came next. I wanted a full life. I wanted to dream about my future. But he took that all away.

There was constant hell in my mind, and it didn't leave room for anything else. I wanted to live, but I couldn't. What I had didn't feel like a life. And I couldn't dream about my future anymore because I didn't see one. It was hard enough just getting through a day or sometimes just an hour. I was in so much pain that it consumed me. It became me. If I wasn't crying about what happened that night, I was crying about how it changed me and how much it hurt. I'd spent so long feeling like this that I didn't know if it would ever stop, and that made me miserable. I didn't want to kill myself. I really didn't. But I didn't know how long I could go on like this. There were dark December nights when I didn't think I would make it to see spring. Those eight months after he touched me were the scariest of my life.

I'd like to tell you I got better, and in some ways I did. I can handle hugs. I can handle people bumping into me. The breakdowns and panic attacks and days of zoning out aren't constant anymore. But they still happen. I don't feel like my suicide is inevitable, but I still think about it sometimes. There's still music I can't listen to and shows I can't watch. It's been at least ten years since her touch, and sometimes I still feel it. Sometimes I stop my girlfriend in the middle of sex because I'm not there anymore, I'm five years old again and I don't want this. It's been a year and a half since his and I still felt a rush of panic last night when a guy put his hand on my arm to help me up after I slipped on the ice. Lately, I've been having awful dreams of getting assaulted, and I spend the next few days feeling lost. I went to someone's house a few weeks ago and some people smoked weed. The smell sent me back to that night, and I cried hysterically the entire drive back to my dorm. I spent this morning watching my trigger band's music videos on YouTube--trying again to gain back some control--and now I feel sick to my stomach.

I'm so tired of being scared and feeling sick and fragile and hiding from the world.

. . .


Less than an hour after running off the ride to get away from my trigger song, another one plays. This one is worse though. Out of all my trigger band's songs, this one affects me the most. Sometimes I try to make myself listen to it because I hate that it has so much power over me, but tonight it wins.

"Babe, where do you want to run to?" my girlfriend asks quickly.

"Anywhere."

She takes my hand, and together we run away again. My heart is pounding, and my eyes are filled with tears. I'm so tired of running.

# The Pretty Things

I am tired of being told
to live in the moment,
to forget the past,
to let go.

The past is not something I hold
onto. It grasps onto me.

It gnaws at my neck, clenches its teeth. Chews
through my red, red veins
as if they were Twizzlers.

I ate Twizzlers at the movies.
So it is no wonder that my life
feels more like watching a movie than
whatever it is life is supposed to feel like.

Somebody must have their finger stuck to the rewind button.

When remembering and forgetting look exactly the same
it is easy for the past to slide into the now
like a baseball player sliding into home
after hearing the crack of your heart
against the slap of a bat

while you are left swallowing dust into your lungs

and pulling splinters from your eyes.

My past knows how to hit real hard without me ever seeing it
coming. It likes to play trick
without ever knowing treat.
It likes to take my breath away, how horrifying
to recognize love in deprivation.

The most loving thing I've ever done for myself
was relearning how to breathe. I relearn
this almost every day and
I still need practice.
There is no spring training for "such basic things"
so sometimes you learn that shit in the unbearable heat
of summertime.

Often, it is not easy to bear witness to your past.

I think about the past
before the past, and I wonder why
that is more acceptable to hold onto.
I guess
people only want the pretty.

But our lives collect dust and scars,
tear stains and blood
and our hands can carry more

than just

the pretty things.

       -Amy Sigle

Don't feel pressured to forgive your abuser.
Some things are unforgivable.

Unforgivable, Emily Harrison-Ach, pen drawing with digital color, 2016.

# Survivor

I don't claim to be a survivor.
It's not righteous to survive,
it's instinct.
What's righteous is to continue to fight,
day after day,
against a world which sees you as broken.
What's righteous is to reawaken your soul,
reach out for help when all trust has been shattered,
to claim this body as yours again.
What's righteous is to use your voice
after having had
your words frozen in your throat,
silenced by shock and fear.
To keep on fighting.
What's righteous is to change
the very structure of your thoughts,
to stop the voices of those who have taught you
that you deserve this pain.
What's righteous is to get beyond just surviving
and to actually be present.
What's righteous is to get up out of bed
each morning
and continue to do the work that it takes
to become whole again.

- Ricki Bloom

# My Trauma looks different from yours (but my healing looks the same)

My trauma looks different than yours
My trauma is wrapped up in churches and prayers and frankincense and myrrh
Tied together with a bow that reads, "This is the only way to salvation"
My trauma looks different than yours
My trauma is all night bible study and speaking in tongues
Being slain in the spirit and baptized in the blood
My trauma looks different than yours
My trauma is hellfire and brimstone and the coming of Christ
Endless repentance in a foolish and desperate attempt to avoid damnation
My trauma looks different than yours
My trauma is thumbs pressed into the palms of my hands outstretched like the crucifix
An unwanted invasion not of my body but of my mind
My trauma looks different from yours

My healing looks the same
My healing is my raised fist at an friend's unexpected touch
The moment I first realized I needed help
My healing looks the same
My healing is messy, days filled with panic attacks and memories that invade my sleep
Resurfacing in my subconscious until I awake with pain from clenching my teeth so tight
My healing looks the same
My healing is loving my body; teaching it how to feel safe
So that the fire alarm in my brain doesn't go off at the mere mention of smoke

My healing looks the same
My healing is Halloween candy and trick or treaters
And for once not thinking about possession and satan
My healing looks the same
My healing is fighting the patriarchy
Embracing my sisters as we recognize that no one, not even god, has
control over us
My healing looks the same
My healing is ongoing, moving, and ever-growing
And while I'll never be the same, I'm stronger now than I was before

My trauma may look different than yours
 But my healing looks the same

                    - Sabrina L. Valente

# Grounded in the Ocean

## Hilda Smith

March 28, 2016

The ocean has always held a place in my heart. The sound of the waves crashing against pebbles, the smell of salt in the air, the spray of foam upon my legs. Waves that seem like they swallow you whole. The chilly embrace that is somehow comforting. Watching the waves eroding what is written in the sand as they crash upon the shore. The heat that seeps into you from sun-warmed sand. The beauty of lost seashells and sand smoothed stones. The ocean has so many comforts to give.

I lost the comfort I found in the ocean when I married my abuser. Instead, I found myself lost in a vast, blue, never-ending, still sea. There were no signs of shore in any direction. Unsure of which way to swim, I clung to my abuser. They acted as a life-boat, one I thought was needed.

But, I just needed the shore. Just a glimpse, and I could get back to the place where the ocean was something I was comforted by.

This was the inspiration for this series of photos. After being away from my family and the town I grew up in, I came home. I went to the beach on a day that was cloudy and drizzling. I walked the shore for hours, taking photos, documenting the sights, smells, and feelings of the ocean.

While many of the photos I took included the ocean, these were the photos that anchored me. They are the pieces of the shore that I can carry with me wherever I go, ensuring that I will always know which direction to swim when I find myself adrift.

Grounded in the Ocean 1 by Hilda Smith, 2016.

Grounded in the Ocean 2, Hilda Smith, 2016.

Grounded in the Ocean 3, Hilda Smith, 2016.

Grounded in the Ocean 4, Hilda Smith, 2016.

# Go Gently

stop blaming yourself
everything is not your fault
let go
forget your past mistakes

find compassion for yourself
offer it to others, too
regret is not your friend
go for it
invite new experiences
volunteer to lift yourself and others up
evade the need to judge your feelings
neither good nor bad
existing
sit with them
set them free

- Jamie Capach

*There are no lingering, invisible handprints on your body.*

Handprints, Emily Harrison-Ach, pen drawing with digital color, 2016.

# These are the things no one tells you about trauma

Claire Biggs

(Originally appeared on the To Write Love on Her Arms blog.)

These are the things no one tells you about trauma:

You become someone who has a before and after. You become someone who has been unmistakably altered.

You become fluent in a different kind of dead language, one that you picked up somewhere you didn't mean to go. It replaces your mother tongue. It falls on deaf ears. The syllables collapse and die in your mouth, a beginning and an ending wrapped in one. You learn that words have a taste, and they taste like shame and regret and guilt and anger. All of them are bitter. I am lucky – yes, *lucky* – to have several friends who speak this same dead language. We found each other and now hold meetings where we utter truths that sound like curses.

You become a foreigner in your own body. A visitor. On your worst days, a hostage. And, of course, you're always the one paying the ransom.

You become someone who believes healing is a word that doesn't apply to you.

You become someone who makes 360-degree turns to ensure you're not being followed or that the person behind you hasn't closed the distance between the two of you since the last time you looked back.

You become someone who locks every door and checks that they're locked every time you walk by.

You become someone who sits with your back against the wall in full view of the exit.

You become someone who panics at the loud noise or the familiar scent.

You become someone who worries when to be on guard. (But that's an easy question when the answer is always.)

You become someone who leaves your back row of seats down so you'll see if anyone is hiding in your car before you unlock it.

You become someone who makes jokes to excuse these behaviors.

You become someone who doesn't find that stuff funny anymore.

These are the things no one understands about trauma:

It is not something you can just move past, but you try anyway. You try to get *over* and *under* and *around* and *through*. It seems to block your way forward at every turn. But you keep trying because there's no such thing as going back.

It is not something that has a reset button. There is no do over. And, worst of all, there's no off switch. It just settles in your chest and threatens to rise in your throat with every breath.

It is not something easily defeated. Sometimes you'll feel like you're playing a game where the odds are stacked against you and where the rules were never explained.

It is not something that lets you pretend you're *all better now*.

These are the things I've learned about trauma:

You can build a *new* after, one you choose for yourself.

You can heal at your own pace, in your own time.

You can find people who will help you along the way.

You can choose what – and who – you become.

You can forgive without forgetting.

You can learn to laugh and love and live again.

You can make it through the unbearable nights and the muted days.

You can move forward even if you don't like what you're carrying with you.

You can move forward even if you don't like what you're leaving behind.

You can move forward.

# Who Gets to Do This Work

Delia Harrington

The presence of so many survivors who are not only willing to tell their story, but to have their name and photo printed in the New York Times next to the words "Sexual assault" and "rape" is phenomenal. It would be completely unbelievable when I first went into crisis in 2012, never mind earlier. I'm particularly cheering for those survivors who have found a way to maintain their own voice and their own autonomy over their story in spite of the media, like Emma Sulkowicz.

We no longer need anyone's permission to matter, to tell our stories, and to be heard.

Still, when I watched *The Hunting Ground*, the part that made me cry was the montage of survivors speaking their names aloud in public, each one clearly about to tell their story to the world, under their own name and face. This is a level of courage that boggles my mind. I am so proud, so moved, and so jealous at the same time. I know that if this is ever published, I will have joined their ranks, but at the time of watching that and writing this, I am still living a life divided. I do some of this work under my own name, but I do it at arm's length. It's the work of an advocate; it's for *other* people, for survivors, for the principle of the thing. I only do the work of an actual survivor anonymously, or with a high degree of danger.

At this point, I've been rolling the dice for a while now. I speak at my alma mater, in towns where my extended family lives, in online forums where I hope no one knows me. I have allowed members of my family, and even some friends who know my perpetrator (but do not know who he is to me) to become involved in the part of my life where I am usually out as a survivor. It's a tightrope that is breaking, fiber by fiber. What happens to me when it finally snaps? What happens to a generation of activists with absolutely no safety net?

For me, some amount of public survivor activism, of named-ness, is inevitable. It's not only who I am, I have simply grown exhausted from living a compartmentalized life. When I can just *be*, without so many walls, restrictions, and excuses, I am softer, quicker to laugh or show any emotion at all, without layers of protective lies and numbness for the feelings to fight through. My survivor-ness and its ramifications weave gently in and out of the conversation and my mind, present only when relevant and bidden upon, not overstaying their welcome or overshadowing the exchange. No one balks, or stammers; no one needs me to comfort them about what happened to me. It is an accepted, often unspoken fact, part of my backstory, so I get to save my words and my energy for what I actually have to say. I am multidimensional, a complete person instead of a single issue incarnate. My edges don't have to be smooth; in fact, no one needs anything of me at all, other than to be who and how I am.

But what about the folks who don't want to be public with anyone? Survivors who *aren't* more at ease when the people around them know? Or the folks who are comfortable with a different level of publicity, a different amount of people knowing? What about the survivors who haven't told their loved ones yet, the kind of loved ones who would be doubly crushed by this information and the fact that we didn't tell them ourselves? Do we speed up our process in one area of our life because we're tired of stalling out in another, an area that seems to require that we make ourselves known? Many survivors just don't want anyone to be able to google their name and find out they're a survivor, and that certainly feels like an appealing level of privacy. Work, in particular, feels like an ideal place to not have part of your life story enter the room before you do, or keep you from even getting in the door. After all, who wants troublemakers? And are we even sure they're even telling the truth? What if they just "rape easy"?

It is so important that survivors have their voice, and that services and policy are determined with us at the center. Nothing for us without us, as they say. But what of all the survivors who can't disclose? Having survivors in the driver's seat is amazing and vital, but we cannot make assumptions about who is and is not a survivor. This creates a pressure on activists, advocates, lobbyists, and caregivers to be an out survivor on top of the valuable public and private work they're already doing. Many folks who aren't survivors are amazing allies in this fight. Sometimes I think we really need those people to be able to shoulder the burdens us survivors can't take. Sometimes I wish more of you would.

Which brings us back to this: why should survivors have to be healing ourselves, fighting for our rights, defending our collective name, and working to prevent more from joining the club all at the same time? We should be listened to, certainly. And for many of us, different aspects of this work is healing. But it's not healing for everyone. Even for those of us it helps, it still sometimes breaks. There are aspects of the work that are too much for us, or times when we simply need to step back. Our voice is important, but so is our well-being. When a person has cancer, their family and friends take up the mantle and fight for better research, better care. The actual patient is only expected to care for themselves. They may go to the walks or fundraisers, but they aren't expected to organize them. Only in these high stigma issues, like racial justice, LGBTQ rights, mental health, and sexual violence are the victims expected to heal themselves while also raising money, writing policy, lobbying legislators, calling out public figures, mobilizing momentum and educating the general public.

For many people, that is daunting. Just *surviving* is daunting. We don't need to add fielding facebook messages from long-forgotten acquaintances when they hear the news to our ever-growing to do lists. For others, it's simply not their skill set, regardless of their willingness or ability to take on the cause at any given time.

Having something shitty happen to you shouldn't make you obligated to do anything at all. In fact, everyone who *hasn't* been violated should be obligated. They've probably got the wherewithal to actually do it, and many of them certainly seem to have opinions about how we do our work. Unfortunately, the way it usually goes is that the people who care about one issue care about them all, and those affected by the majority of injustices do the lion's share of this work.

Our voices need to be heard, but the pressure to be an out, activist survivor sometimes feels like too much to me. The trade-off is enormous: giving up your privacy and (possibly) your dignity in exchange for what? More tired nights, more people telling you their shitty opinion, more people relying on you to save them from ever becoming like you? What do you say if someone questions your tactics or knowledge, but you're not an out survivor? Do you out yourself in order to have your opinion be seen as more valid?

Outing yourself as a survivor takes its toll, but so does keeping that in. Every day I have to deny a piece of myself. But I don't just keep quiet to protect myself from social stigma or online harassment, or to prevent the inevitable inundation of comments from everyone in my life. I do it to make myself more palatable to others. I do it so I don't have to be The Survivor 100% of the time, and so I don't have to speak for all survivors. I do it so I don't ruin your barbecue (whoops) or bring everybody down during Truth or Dare. I do it so I don't have to comfort you about my assault, so you won't dismiss my opinion as biased, and so I don't have to keep depleting myself by having these conversations. I keep quiet so my grandparents' hearts don't have to break, so my sweet cousin doesn't yet have to know the full force of evil in the world, and because I just don't have the energy to take on everyone's pain in addition to my own.

Distancing myself from my fellow survivors may be the worst part. They are not some abstract concept, and neither am I. They are not *other people*, they are *my* people. They are the only ones who consistently hold me up. They are the angels on my shoulders, propelling me forward with their love. To deny that we are the same, to set them apart as the pitiable other, to deny that I am one of them, is to deny that love, the love that keeps me alive.

What if you can't out yourself because you're not a survivor? There are many allies who have a more comprehensive view of what survivors need because they're not caught up in the shame and self-hate that so often accompany our assaults. Sometimes the harshest things I hear are coming out of survivors' mouths, my own included. We forget that there are others around to hear it, including other survivors and less knowledgeable bystanders. We figure that if we, the survivor, aren't offended, that no one else has a right to be. But that's not really how it works. Sometimes only an ally can remind us of that.

So does this work only belong to the survivors willing to lash themselves to the front of the ship? Those who can withstand the consequences, the online harassment, the googling potential employers, the last-minute date cancellations, the enduring memory of the internet, and the inescapable stigma of a thing the rest of humanity let happen, over and over again, to so very many of us? Do we just have to add the ramifications of stigma-laden public service to the ever-growing list of burdens survivors are expected to bear?

I don't know the answer to any of this. It's what keeps me stagnant in my healing, vacillating between fear and a profound desire to move forward. I marinate in the knowledge that 'forward' is bound to be an inhospitable place, and a deep and abiding anger that I even have to contemplate any of this at all.

## Why I Do This

For many people, the most unfathomable part of my story is the fact that I tell it. The work I choose to do around the issue of sexual violence, and the way I make my contributions, sort of blows people's minds. Over the years, many have expressed concern, although those who didn't know why were usually the most vocal. I suppose they couldn't fathom embroiling yourself in this world if you didn't have to, and hoped I would use my presumed privilege to escape the brutal truth.

I do this work because I can. Not everyone is in a position to donate their time or money. There was a time when, in my eyes, volunteering with BARCC (Boston Area Rape Crisis Center) or going to their annual Walk for Change would have linked me too closely with this issue; someone might know. There are a billion reasons to not be able to speak publicly about this, volunteer to run events, spread the word, or raise money. To name a few: a lack of time or money, the subject matter being overwhelming, fear of being outed by oneself or another, or just a straight up unwillingness to lay this shit bare. These are all good and valid reasons to not do this work, and to not do it this way, and no one should ever feel bad about them.

I do this work because I'm good at it. I have been good at public speaking my whole life. I have always loved storytelling, and one way or another it has been a huge part of my career. I know how to craft messages, spread the word, run events, raise money, and change minds. This is my wheelhouse, my bread and butter. This is my stage, my jam, my hill to die on.

I do this work for all of the survivors who can't. I also do this type of work because we're all doing something, whether it's writing letters to congress, posting on social media, calling out victim-blaming in conversation, passing on resources, or simply refusing to let our assault define us. I firmly believe that it is up to each of us to walk our own path, and when that is all put together, it adds up to a movement that is beautiful and strong. There have been things I cannot or will not do over the years, and there was always someone else who had that strength, and that type of strength, someone who stepped up.

I remember telling my support group that I wanted to join BARCC's Survivor Speaker Bureau, and they were surprised and a bit in awe. On our last night of group therapy, we all went around and told each other how we felt, how we watched one another grow, and how we were inspired by each other. When it came time for the group to talk about me, almost every person told me how proud they were, knowing I was going out into the world to speak on behalf of us all. Some even apologized for not being able to do it themselves. They told me how they admired my activism and my voice, that they felt better knowing that I would be representing us, pushing and fighting for us.

So that's what I do. Whenever someone asks why I do this work during a speaking engagement, talking about my support group is the one part where I get choked up. I think of all of these inspiring, varied, fierce people who refuse to be made small by someone else's cruelty. I remember that they are right behind me, the angels on my shoulders propelling me forward with their strength and love. I think of all the qualities I wish I could borrow from them: their anger, their stability, their loving romantic relationships, their access to their own emotions, their sense of their own bodies and selves. I'm grateful to be able to throw my activism and my voice into the shared pool of collective strength.

I do this work because it's the right thing to do and because I enjoy it. I feel compelled. Not out of guilt or misplaced anxiety, but out of a desire to make as many lives safer, and experiences easier, as I can. I think of the pantheon of people who helped me, and I pay it forward. I raise the money to pay for my services, and the services of those who cannot fundraise. I talk to newbie survivors who have no one, to bring them in from them cold so they may have kind words and be connected to services years before I was. I publicly assert my opinions and values on the issue, so there will be fewer people who innocently hold wrongheaded beliefs, and so the shitty people who hold them on purpose won't have a crowd to hide in. I tell my story so that people can learn that it can happen to anyone. I do it so they can ask me all the tough questions, saving the survivors in their lives from having to answer them while in crisis, and to make sure they know what to do and say when someone they love eventually discloses to them.

I do this work because it's who I am. I have always been an activist and a rabble-rouser. I often say if I had cancer, we would all be doing walks and making t-shirts. So why not with this? Being myself about this aspect of my life is normalizing. It reminds me that this is just as not-my-fault as MS is not my uncle's fault. It shows that this cannot change me, cannot take my voice away from me. I do this because I've still got some fight left in me, and I'm going to use every last bit of it to care for myself and others. I'm fighting to create the world we deserve to live in, even if our world doesn't deserve us yet.

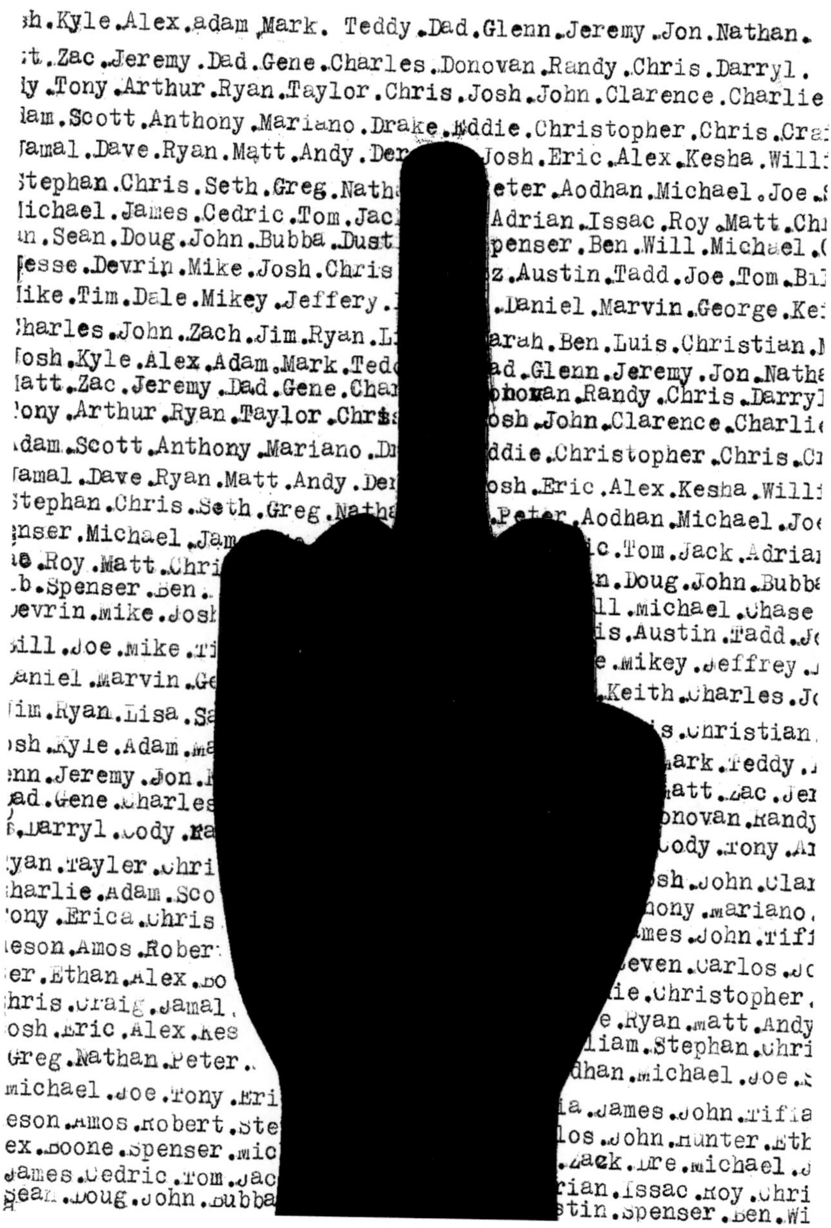


#MeToo by Darci McFarland & dozens of survivor friends, 2017.